Planted In Purpose
WHAT'S FEEDING YOUR ROOTS?

SallyAnn Gray

Planted In Purpose
WHAT'S FEEDING YOUR ROOTS?

Judge a tree by the fruit it bears not by the fruit it talks about, promises or professes. You can tell how serious you are not by what you say, but by what you do! Act on your dreams. Do that which you are called to do. If not you, who? If not now, when?

SallyAnn Gray

In the words of the late Myles Monroe-

"God does not cause anything to begin that is not already finished." Therefore, the fact that you are born means that you are a finished product. Everything you need to do your life's work has already been downloaded in you. If you dream it; if God has already shown it to you, then it's already done. All you are required to do is believe and be obedient through the process. It is already done!

Planted In Purpose
WHAT'S FEEDING YOUR ROOTS?

Jeremiah 17:7-8

*7 "But blessed is the one who trusts in the L<small>ORD</small>,
whose confidence is in him.
8 They will be like a tree planted by the water
that sends out its roots by the stream.
It does not fear when heat comes;
its leaves are always green.
It has no worries in a year of drought
and never fails to bear fruit."*

SallyAnn Gray

PLANTED IN PURPOSE: WHAT'S FEEDING YOUR ROOTS?

Copyright @ 2018 SallyAnn Gray

All rights reserved. No part of this publication may be reproduced, stored in a retrieval system or transmitted in any form or by any means- electronic, mechanical, photocopying, recording, or any other- except for brief quotations in printed reviews, without the prior permission of the publisher. All scripture quotations are from the Holy Bible, King James or New International Version.

ISBN-13: 978-1-949343-15-1
ISBN-10: 1-949343-15-4
SallyAnn Gray Kingston, Jamaica

Illustrations by Mark Gray
Pictures by Mark Gray
Cover Design by Mark Gray
Edited by Tamara Francis
Printed in the United States

Visit us at www.SallyAnnGraySpeaks.com
Facebook: SallyAnnSpeaks
Instagram: @@SallyAnnSpeaks
Twitter: @SallyAnnSpeaks
Email: SallyAnnGraySpeaks@outlook.com

DEDICATION

*This book is dedicated to my supportive and loving husband Mr. Mark Gray. I have watched him, despite many challenges, decide to not only be planted in his purpose, but mind the soil his roots are planted in. Without speaking much, he has shown consistency and resilience which has managed to filter into my soil.
I love you baby.*

CONTENTS

Acknowledgments xi

Preface xiii

Chapter 1 Truth vs. Lies 1

Chapter 2 Seeds vs. Sowing 9

Chapter 3 Intention vs. Plan of Action 29

Chapter 4 Rooted vs. Planted 43

Chapter 5 Here vs. There 53

Chapter 6 Tools vs. Theory 59

Contributors 77

    What does it mean to be Planted in Purpose? 79

Final Message from Author 95

ACKNOWLEDGMENTS

To the Holy Spirit for revealing every word on every page, I say thank You for partnering with me, for without You, God's work could never be done in and through me.

To my husband Mark, who has been my ever support since I started this journey of renewal and becoming planted in my God given purpose. This book is dedicated to you because every day I observe you plant yourself in your God-given purpose and remain rooted in the things of God. I know that He is feeding your roots and I am giving God thanks for your level of commitment and dedication to what you are called to do. Thank you for being a source of inspiration to me.

To my handsome son, Malachi and beautiful daughter, Sarah: you are the salt of the earth, light of the world and God made you to make a difference. I am eternally grateful to God for the privilege of being your mother.

To my sisters in Christ who have contributed to this book by sharing what it means for them to be Planted in Purpose, I love you guys. Thank you, Shakobie, Kedesha, Wanda, Madlyn, Genee, Crystal, Sherie and Alderene. You all have a special place in my heart and have helped to keep me planted and rooted in my purpose. I love you all very much.

To you, the reader, every one of you means so much to me. I know how hard it is to become planted in purpose. I know how hard it is to remain rooted in the things of Christ in today's age of social media. We are constantly being bombarded with so much and it can sometimes distort our faith in God. My encouragement to you is: focus on the things that are good and of good report. Only apples can come from an apple tree; therefore, if you focus on God, only the things of God can come.

PREFACE

You know your purpose, you have identified your talents, and you have started doing the things God has called you to do. Now you are weary, you have stopped in your tracks. You have tried everything to get your energy back and it's not working. The book you started, is still stuck at chapter four. You registered the business, but you have failed in your attempts to get it off the ground. You opened the restaurant but for one reason or another, business is slow and now, you just don't know if this dream is worth it for you anymore. You are enthusiastic about an upcoming project, something you know the Lord has called you to do; but the cynical remarks from loved ones have left you feeling discouraged. Now you are wondering, what's the use?

We have all been there, I was there during the process of writing this book. Stuck at chapter four for a long time, distracted and full of anxiety because I did not know how to get back on track. Planted in Purpose in Christ is a journey that helps people who have been planted in their purpose remain rooted in it. The truth is, we can't try to do anything in life. Either we do it or we don't. This, my friend, is the first lesson to being Planted in your Purpose. Either you are in it or you are not.

How well we carry out our life's work, is totally dependent on the quality of the soil we become rooted in. What's really feeding your roots? What tools can you utilize to **start right and finish strong**? You know the saying *'many are called but few are chosen.'* Some start the race but few cross the finish line.

Join me as we journey together through the intricacies that prevent many of us from finishing our course. Join me as we uncover the tools that will enable you to become so rooted in your destiny that nothing will move you. Not rain, not snow, not sleet, **not anything**. This is a journey that shows how you can remain PLANTED In PURPOSE. This journey shows you how to manage what feeds your roots. Your life depends on it!

There are some basic questions that every human being must answer to be fulfilled in this life:

1) Who am I?
2) Where am I from?
3) What are my talents?
4) What is my life's work?
5) What am I going to do about it?
6) How will I finish my course?
7) What is God's will for my life?

Who am I? speaks to your identity and lineage. If you don't know who you are, you will quickly be someone else. *Where am I from?* speaks to your heritage. *Why am I here?* is a question of purpose and impact you were meant to have. *What are my talents?* speaks directly to gifts you have been given. *What is my life's work?* speaks to your potential. What am I going to do about it? speaks to your plan, strategy and the execution. *Where am I going?* speaks to your destiny, your assignment, your life's work. Your purpose is already in you. You are already a complete product, manufactured and designed by Jesus Christ himself. Everything you need to function in this life was already downloaded in you.

It has happened to us all before, we start something and cannot seem to finish it. What do we do then? How do we apply biblical principles to stay planted in our purpose? Where do we go? Who do we turn to for help? I assert to you that the best business partner is the Holy Spirit.

In April 2017 I launched my career as a transformational speaker. I was very concerned about many things. What will people think? How will they react? After all, to those who knew me back when, it would naturally come as a shock that I could be a source of inspiration to others. The funny thing is, God specializes in using the ones among us who have been rejected by man to do His work. We cannot comprehend the ways of God. My advice is, don't, just be obedient.

Little did I know that I, considered by many as the least among them, the foolish thing of the world, would be chosen by God to do the work I am doing now. I strongly believe that there are many "least among them" out there. I believe there are many "foolish things of the world," that God has appointed to minister to others. I believe that is you.

You are a seed. God created you and placed everything you need in you! There is no life without purpose. Think about it, if you sprinkled salt on your food and it did not give flavor, what would be its purpose. Similarly, if you live your life, without doing your life's work, what would be the purpose of your existence?

Chapter 1

Truth vs. Lies

John 8:31-32

To the Jews who had believed him, Jesus said, "If you hold to my teaching, you are really my disciples. Then you will know the truth, and the truth will set you free."

For a very long time I believed every single lie the enemy told me. Even as I write this book, I am in a constant warfare to replace lies with truth. The lies that held me captive for so long, still rear their ugly head today. Even at age thirty-seven, with all I know, I still struggle. I want you to know this is something we absolutely can work on together. This battle is spiritual. Things that are seen have very little to do with what we are facing, do not believe the lies of the enemy. Yes, that same lie you have believed all along about yourself, dispose of it. Know that you are fearfully and wonderfully made. Know that He died for you. Know that His promises are pure and true. If He said it, you can believe it. The enemy is cunning and will have us balled up in a fetal position drenched in his stupid lies. The truth is, there is a way to become aware of the lies, and that is our strength. With awareness we can identify where we are at. With awareness we can use tools to get us to where we need to be.

Guess what? The enemy knows his purpose, which is to kill, steal and destroy. It's in your best interest to know yours, which is to live, have and build up others. To live, we must go to our true source. He came that we may have life and have it more abundantly. Irrespective of what is said about religion and spirituality; at some point, on your own, without external influence, you must reconcile the infallible word of God as truth. Without that resolute peace in what you believe, the enemy will toss you about in a flurry of confusion. Nobody can work or be productive in confusion. God is not the author of it. He thrives in a peaceful environment. At the top of the list as you become planted in your purpose is finding truth and finding peace in that truth.

What are some essential TRUTHS about God:

1) He loves
2) He forgives
3) He saves
4) He redeems
5) He gives grace

Soak up pure biblical truth through your roots. It gives strength to the weak and provides comfort on the day of affliction. Without resolute truth and belief in what your maker says, the enemy will keep your mind embattled long enough. Long enough that you may never realize or walk in your purpose. I say find the truth and become resolute about it.

For me, the statement "I am the way, the truth and the life," is as real as truth gets. Jesus Christ said it and I will not dispute it. He came, He lived, He died and He arose. That settles it for me. With that truth, I go forward knowing **who** I am. I stand firm in my abilities, gifts, talents and purpose. Not because I am so 'great' but because I now know that He who began a good work in me will complete it.

Know the truth, believe the truth, digest the truth and the truth will set you free. You will be free from every lie the enemy told you. The same ones he told me, lies such as:

- You are unworthy
- You are ugly
- Nobody likes you
- You don't fit in
- Nobody cares about you
- You are not special

Look at the cover of this book, the girl that looks so poised and confident, yes her. The enemy told me so many lies. I am replacing them with TRUTH. Please don't let me do it alone. The TRUTH is:

- You are fearfully and wonderfully made
- You are His handiwork
- You are special
- You have purpose in you
- You are loved
- You have a testimony
- You have special gifts and talents
- You have everything you need inside you. The rod is in your hand.

Starting on the journey of purpose requires a renewed strength and renewed WILL. You must first be planted in the divine will of God. His will is the truth. Staying the course and being PLANTED in it requires TRUTH. You must know it, you must believe it and most importantly you must act on it. Even on the days when TRUTH eludes you in the physical realm. Do what Ephesians 6:14 says "Stand therefore, having your loins girt about with TRUTH." Clothe yourself in His truth, when you do so, LIES cannot take root.

There is another truth that we tend to forget, the truth about ourselves. Many of us have business meetings all day but forget to have the most important meeting we need; a frank meeting with ourselves. My meetings with myself were brutal, to say the least. I had to face myself on several things. It was hard and yours will be hard too. Do the work and get to the TRUTH so you can plant yourself where you need to be.

There is no TRYING to do this. Either you do, or you don't. Do me a favor where you are right now. Try to sit on a chair. You just try it. Either you sit, or you stand. There is no TRYING to sit in a chair and there is no TRYING to walk in PURPOSE. Do the work so you can get started. Make the SHIFT right now. Decide if you are going to believe the truth or believe the lies. Decide if you will sit or stand and decide NOW.

Planted in Purpose in Christ

Journal Entry 1

List some lies the enemy has told you about your life	List the TRUTH you will use to replace the lies

Take some time to reflect on the ways you will replace LIES with TRUTH. You are in control of your mind. Ask yourself, how will I act on this every day? How will I capture lies and replace them with truth for the next seven days?

_____

_____

_____

_____

_____

_____

_____

_____

_____

_____

_____

_____

_____

_____

_____

CHAPTER 2

Seed vs. Sowing

2 Corinthians 9:6

Remember this: Whoever sows sparingly will also reap sparingly, and whoever sows generously will also reap generously.

The sower (which is you) sows the seeds. God's Word is the seed and a man's heart is the ground. If your heart is not able to protect and keep the seed, it cannot manifest. In other words, we must put the Word to work in our lives. If you do not see what God has promised you in your life, check the condition of your heart, eyes and mouth. What is in your heart? What do you allow to enter your mind through your eyes? What are you speaking with your tongue? This has been a struggle for me. I have many struggles with my little tongue.

The times in my life when I was seeing things I did not like around me, I examined not only what I was thinking but I examined what my mouth was saying. Many times, I was praying in one breath but destroying my own future with my very own tongue in another breath. There were times when I would be praying to God for a house but saying out my very own mouth that I could not find the down payment. It is important for us to protect the Word, study the Word, speak the Word and the naturally we will see the Word. You must put the Word to work. I truly decided in my mind that I would not be one of those believers who destroyed my own future with my own mouth. Work the Word and the Word will work for you.

In an effort to contextualize this concept, it is important to examine the heart condition. The condition of the heart is very important because it prevents or produces what we want to see in our lives.

Way side heart

In the wayside heart, the Word is sown but because the hearer did not understand it, the seed was not planted deep enough to take root. Let me pause here and explain how important it is to understand what you are hearing and seeing. For every aspect of your life, getting wisdom and understanding is paramount. If you remember nothing else from this Chapter, remember to get understanding, it will save your life. I got my degree in hard knocks because I was too impatient and way too jumpy in decision making. My husband is different, he says very little, thinks a lot and examines all sides of something before making a decision. On the other hand, I used my emotions to make decisions. Needless to say, I'm not the chief decision maker in the household and with good reason.

Learn from me, get understanding on all things because understanding undergirds wisdom. For practical application, don't just take a job opportunity because it looks good. Every GOOD thing is not always a GOD thing. Examine the contract, the benefits, if something is not clear, get clarity before making an emotional decision which may not be the best decision for you or your family.

Stony heart or ground

In the case of the stony heart; people hear the Word, understand the Word and receive the Word. Even though the Word is received, it is not deeply rooted. The litmus test for this heart is how the individual responds on the day of affliction. If life is good they believe. If things get bad, they breakdown and forget the promises of God. One Word here is RELATIONSHIP. Have a relationship with God for yourself. If the Word is not deeply rooted, this person loses their joy and peace at a moment's notice.

I was this person for the first two years of my Christian walk. After hearing a good sermon, I would be on a spiritual high until my co-worker started the rubbish on Monday morning. Then it's back to being stressed, complaining and not wanting to be bothered. Take it from me, having conditional faith is not what God intends for us. To be planted in purpose, the Word must take serious root in our heart.

What you are rooted in, will preserve you on the day of trouble. This means if you root yourself in social media, social media will preserve you on the day of affliction. Do you get the point?

Thorn filled heart/ground

The person with the thorn filled heart, gets the Word, understands the Word but is not focused on the Word. I could easily be placed in this category from time to time because I get distracted at times. What I now know is that focus and attention needs to be given to the Word. We cannot allow our attention to be given to the circumstances around us.

Instead of studying the Word, we get distracted by things like Facebook and Instagram, busy looking at what everybody else is doing, rather than focusing on what we should be doing. We must meditate on the Word. When we lose focus on the Word, whatever we are focusing on enters the heart and chokes the Word. Therefore, we must be careful what we watch, what we listen to and who we surround ourselves with.

If you are working on your purpose, stay focused on YOUR calling and stay focused on YOUR assignment. Do not let distractions choke the vision and abort it prematurely. No root, no focus, no harvest, no fruit, **no NOTHING**. Get back to the basics and **FOCUS**.

Good heart or good ground

People with this kind of heart hear the Word and accept it, no negotiating, no debating. They study it and mediate on it. God's Word is it for them. They are resolute. People with this heart thrive in purpose because they know whose they are. Their roots run deep in the Word and suck nutrients from their RELATIONSHIP with God. Not the RELIGION and TRADITIONS they were raised in. They know the truth and are not easily swayed.

As you plant yourself in purpose, it is important to know what kind of heart you possess. The posture of your heart during your journey has everything to do with how it will end. To be planted in purpose in Christ, the posture of the heart must be right.

A seed is anything that when sown, you will get something bigger than that which was sown. A harvest is what you receive after a period of sowing. If you plant a seed in the ground, the soil must be right. For us, our soil is what surrounds us while we grow and mature in purpose. Then there is the maintenance of the seed in the ground such as exposure to sunlight and water. Be mindful of who and what you entertain especially in the early stages of purpose. The seed, if maintained properly, will produce a harvest of fruit. If the roots are deep down enough in the ground, the fruit will be potent, rich, sweet and effective. The fruit will be vibrant and the fruit will multiply. Simply put, if you plant yourself in God and allow your roots to suck nutrients from HIM, when you start to walk in purpose, you will be effective and have the desired impact.

Trees produce after its kind, if you are planted in CHRIST, your fruit will be like CHRIST. Apple seeds will never produce grapes as its fruit. Similarly, if your seed is the WORD and you plant yourself in the things of God, the fruit you bare must image all things CHRIST. It's a biblical, scientific and practical principle. Your harvest depends on and responds to the seeds you sow, **ALWAYS!**

Sow the seed which is the WORD. Plant yourself in purpose which is the WORD. Stay rooted by consistently studying and surrounding yourself with all things WORD. Bear good fruit which is a natural result of being planted and rooted in the WORD. You will flourish where you are planted because of the WORD.

Recognize your current season for what it is and always keep your eyes on the WORD. Even when your reality looks different from the WORD, speak the things that are not as though they were, because that is in the WORD. If you do these things you will BLOOM where you are planted. This is not some fairy tale fix, it is something I have lived. Whenever I started to lose my way, I zoned back into my RELATIONSHIP with God and what He had to say about me.

One thing I have learnt is to be sensitive to seasons, misalignment causes frustration. If you are in a new season, it may require you to sow differently. A new season calls for a new strategy. This means if God has expanded your territory by giving you a new job with more responsibility, it requires new strategy within the family dynamics. Nothing is wrong with summer clothes, but if you wear it during the winter, you are setting yourself up to get sick.

It is important to assess whether, the new activity or seed being sown is taking place in the correct season. I refer to this as SEASONAL ALIGNMENT. Ever so often, it is important to conduct a purpose analysis to ensure we are doing the right things at the right time. It is essential to be careful of doing the right things in the wrong dimension.

Planted in Purpose in Christ

Journal Entry 2

When I sit and reflect on the condition of my heart or soil, I can honestly say my heart is _____.

Reflect on some of the things that prevent your heart from being fertile ground for God to use you mightily. Document them below.

_____
_____
_____
_____
_____
_____
_____
_____
_____
_____
_____
_____
_____
_____
_____
_____
_____
_____
_____

Seasonal Alignment

Where am I now?

Where do I want to be?

Where does God want me to be? How will I know?

What season of purpose am I in?

Am I doing the right things in this season?

Are some things pre-mature and others long overdue?

What am I doing about it today?

What is my life's work (my contribution to the planet)?

Do you have a vision and mission?

As it relates to PURPOSE, where do you see yourself one year from now?

_____
_____
_____
_____
_____
_____
_____
_____
_____
_____
_____
_____
_____
_____
_____
_____
_____
_____
_____
_____
_____
_____
_____
_____
_____
_____
_____

CHAPTER 3

Intention vs. Plan of Action

James 1:23-25

Anyone who listens to the word but does not do what it says is like someone who looks at his face in a mirror and, after looking at himself, goes away and immediately forgets what he looks like. But whoever looks intently into the perfect law that gives freedom and continues in it— not forgetting what they have heard, but doing it, they will be blessed in what they do.

Everyone, including me, wants the promise but few of us want to go through the process. The process does not have to be perceived as painful if you understand the purpose of it: to make you stronger, to transform you into the person you need to be to carry out your life's work.

What are you willing to do to walk boldly in your purpose? Few people embrace the process that takes them to the promised land. To get to the promise you must accept the process. To determine if the process is worth it for you, ask yourself this question:

What makes life worth living for me? _____
_____

Is it your dreams, your children, a spouse, parents, could it be your purpose in Christ? Each of us, whether we admit it or not, know that there is a higher calling on our lives.

I ran for a very long time from my calling which is really evangelism. It took such a long time for me to even say it out of my mouth that God had great work for me to do because I was fearful of what I had to give up. Is that you today? Based on my very own experience, there is very little fulfillment outside the will of God. Stop running, start accepting. It's hard but necessary.

What is your WHY? Your why will make action meaningful and will determine how you live this life. There is no need in me boosting you up. You must be convinced. That SHIFT must take place in your own mind. The only reason people

TAKE ACTION is if they are convinced of the IMPACT the action will have.

If you are not seeing the results you want in your life, it is because you are not taking enough consistent action to see them manifested. This was such a hard truth for me to face. My health goal has long been a struggle. Going to the gym once a week and eating whatever I wanted did not exactly get me the Halle Berry body I was going for. The body I desired required action that I was simply not focused enough to take. The result was a pudge belly and love handles. That was not much fun. I share that to make clear that many are the plans of a man's heart but if there is no meaningful action aimed at achieving the plans, then it's just a wish. Wishful thinking never got anyone anywhere.

For anything meaningful to take place, especially on matters of purpose, these are the steps I suggest:

1) Believe it (Be resolute about your purpose)
2) Say it (Your words are seeds sown into the atmosphere)
3) Strategize (Create a vision, mission and goals around what you believe)
4) Create an action plan
5) Take the action steps

Words are the seeds sown into the atmosphere. Once sown, follow with the requisite action and watch the promises of God unfold. How you think determines how you feel and how you feel determines how you act. When these align with God's perfect will for your life, you will be planted in purpose and rooted in the TRUTH, which is the Word of God.

Planted in Purpose in Christ
Journal Entry 3

> ***Planted Tip:***
>
> *Being planted in purpose means you have to walk through a process. Being rooted in purpose means that intention must become a plan. Walking in purpose means that the plan must become action. Staying in purpose means your roots must be firmly rooted in unshakable faith and trust in God to finish the work He started in you. It is a God thing not a YOU thing.*

This exercise will reveal some deep things for you. Don't rush it, don't move past it, answer the questions and give them deep thought. You cannot become planted in your purpose unless you decide to take meaningful action.

Do you have a relationship with God?

_____
_____
_____
_____
_____
_____
_____
_____
_____

Are you connected to like-minded men and women of God?

_____
_____
_____
_____
_____
_____
_____
_____
_____
_____
_____

What really makes life meaningful for you?

_____
_____
_____
_____
_____
_____
_____
_____
_____
_____
_____
_____

What gives you a sense of purpose?

_____
_____
_____
_____
_____
_____
_____
_____
_____
_____
_____

What is your God-given purpose?

Pocket of Wisdom: Purpose is given by God, therefore despite any leadership seminar, motivational session or summits you have attended, purpose can only be revealed to you by the Holy Spirit and confirmation sent by a man of God. Do not be deceived. In addition, it is every believers purpose to spread the gospel of Jesus Christ and in so doing help to build up the Kingdom.

_____
_____
_____
_____
_____

What have you done about it to this point?

Do you regret not acting on something in your life?

_____
_____
_____
_____
_____
_____
_____
_____
_____
_____
_____
_____
_____

Do you fear anything? If yes, list them.

1) _____
2) _____
3) _____
4) _____
5) _____
6) _____
7) _____

What is your plan for confronting the things you fear?

Document the plan

What does taking action really mean to you?

What is the goal of the plan?

What are the action steps?

How will I move from intention to plan?

How will I move from action to seeing results?

_____
_____
_____
_____
_____
_____
_____
_____
_____
_____
_____
_____

How committed am I to taking-action starting right now?

_____
_____
_____
_____
_____
_____
_____
_____
_____
_____
_____
_____

What would my life look like in the next 6 months, if I took no action towards my goals?

_____
_____
_____
_____
_____
_____
_____
_____
_____
_____
_____

Based on your answers to the above questions, can you afford to not act?

_____
_____
_____
_____
_____
_____
_____
_____
_____
_____
_____

CHAPTER 4

Rooted vs. Planted

Jeremiah 17:8

They will be like a tree planted by the water that sends out its roots by the stream. It does not fear when heat comes; its leaves are always green. It has no worries in a year of drought and never fails to bear fruit."

You can be planted in anything but how rooted you are depends on your environment and the quality of your soil. Every strong and tall tree was once a seed. Before the seed became a tree, it had to be nourished with sunlight, food and water for sustenance. Even before the tree broke ground and became visible to the physical eye, its roots went deep down in the earth as it became strengthened, knowing all the while that the deeper its roots, the stronger it would be when it broke ground. How we react to the storms of life depends on how deep our roots are.

A young root can only become a mature root depending on the soil its planted in. This means the conditions of the soil must be conducive to facilitate growth of the seed. Further to that, the baby root hair must be deliberate in sucking up water and nutrients from the good soil. This facilitates the producing of good fruit.

The diagram below shows perfectly what it looks like when a seed is planted in the ground. There are many things that take place for it to become rooted enough to emerge as a big, tall and stable tree.

ROOTED	PLANTED
Being rooted means to grow down or establish deeply and firmly.	Planted means to put a seed in the ground, set or place in a particular position.

What does this diagram represent for you? I invite you to take some time to reflect.

_____
_____
_____
_____
_____
_____
_____
_____
_____
_____

My interpretation is that a young root can only become a mature root depending on the soil it is planted in. This means the conditions of the soil must be conducive to facilitate growth of the seed.

What does this mean for you? Simply put if you are a baby in PURPOSE, you must first assess your environment to determine if it is a growth environment or a stunting environment.

Of course, what you listen to, watch and people you surround yourself with all make up your environment. Iron sharpens iron, if your iron is dull then your environment is dull. My entire life changed when I assessed my environment and the people in it.

To be rooted, we must apply what we know. Knowing a lot without applying a lot is a recipe to staying stunted, to staying in seed form and to staying stagnant.

Pocket of Wisdom: Everything of significance, everything that is in alignment with God's perfect will for our life; happens by partnering with the Holy Spirit, in our own strength, we are weak and ineffective.

I learnt this hard lesson when I tried to write this very book you are reading in my own strength. It was not until I submitted the project to the Lord's direction that these fingers started typing something that made any kind of sense.

To become rooted:

1. **Make a plan;** we must write all our visions and make it plain. Without a vision the people shall perish
2. **Submit the plan to the Lord;** this means pray and fast about it
3. **Take action;** when God gives the directive via confirmation you proceed
4. **Be consistent; faint not**, you cannot stop because you encounter a problem, you must keep doing
5. **Stay faithful**
6. **Stay prayerful**

Stay ROOTED; come what may, you never give up on the promises of God. I mean it could rain for a year, you still train. It could be snowing outside, you must still work.

When God plants you in a plan, you must take the steps to become rooted in His plan for your life. Many are called but few are chosen. The chosen ones among us are the rooted ones among us. If God places something in your spirit and you don't act on it, it will be hard for Him to accomplish His plans for your life through you. You must be willing, and you must submit. It's not easy but it's necessary if you want to reap real, long lasting peace and fulfillment.

If you want to know what's feeding your roots, just check your fruits.

LAW: FROM ROOT TO FRUIT

Planted in Purpose in Christ
Journal Entry 4

Am I planted?

_____
_____
_____
_____
_____
_____
_____
_____
_____
_____

Am I rooted?

_____
_____
_____
_____
_____
_____
_____
_____
_____
_____
_____

What am I rooted in?

_____
_____
_____
_____
_____
_____
_____
_____
_____
_____

Am I growing?

_____
_____
_____
_____
_____
_____
_____
_____
_____
_____

Am I bearing fruits?

CHAPTER 5

Here vs. There

Jeremiah 29:11

For I know the thoughts that I think toward you, saith the Lord, thoughts of peace, and not of evil, to give you an expected end.

As we become planted in purpose, there are some things that will get us to purpose, and others that won't. If we look at the story of the Israelites in the wilderness, we see that three major things prevented them from entering the Promised Land.

- Lack of Faith
- Lack of Obedience
- Constant Complaining

To enter your Promised Land, you must leave your season of bondage behind (whatever that may be for you). To walk in your destiny and enter your Promised Land, it becomes essential do the opposite of the Israelites. You must:

- Be Full of Faith
- Act in Obedience
- Have an attitude of Gratitude in all Seasons

When we experience trying times in our life, it is easier said than done to be full of gratitude. The truth is, we can choose the way of complaining and being miserable about everything because everything in life is a choice. The question I would pause to ask here is; how is that working for you?

How do we remain faithful during life's difficulties? Being faithful does not mean that we never experience moments of doubt. It means we become accustomed to God working things together for us, that after a period of difficulty we become confident that it too will pass. We start to develop the confidence in His ability to fix it rather than our choice to stress over it. Faith is like a muscle developed over time. The more we exercise it, the stronger it becomes.

When God gives us a vision, it is necessary to hold on to it irrespective of what people say or what things look like in the natural. The truth is, it is our responsibility to be planted and remain rooted in our purpose. The sooner we understand and accept that our purpose is for us to fulfill, the quicker we can get down to business. The quicker we can stop seeking approval from people who can't catch the vision. The quicker we stop sucking nutrients from things designed to contaminate our roots and kill our tree.

Planted in Purpose
Journal Entry 5

What attitudes do you have which prevent you from walking in purpose?

_____
_____
_____
_____
_____
_____
_____
_____
_____

What attitudes do you have which can enhance you on your journey to fulfilling your purpose?

_____
_____
_____
_____
_____
_____
_____
_____
_____

Do you have a network of people who can help you hold on to the vision God has given you?

Chapter 6

Tools vs Theory

Everybody knows a lot but the only way to get ahead in life is if we do what we know. There comes a time when we must shift from knowing to doing. If you are among the two percent of people on the planet who commit to doing more than you know, this toolkit is for you. As you plant yourself in your purpose and as you advance from season to season, these tools can be used to help you stay planted and rooted in what God has called you to do.

TRANSFORMATION TOOLKIT

The purpose of a toolkit is that the tool will be utilized properly at the appropriate time. It is suggested therefore that you draw for these tools at the appropriate timing, in the correct season and at the right time.

TOOL 1 - GET FOCUSED

Be focused, if you don't know where you are going, any road will take you there. When you become planted in purpose and when you become clear about your vision, life gets simple. It becomes easy for you to say no to people, places and things that do not align or agree with the vision. Get focused, don't try to be a jack of all trades and master of none. Commit to one thing at a time and commit to doing it well.

TOOL 2 - BE TRUE TO YOU

Know who you are, and don't you dare wait on anyone to affirm your greatness. You are a star, just shine. Hold the vision and don't let negative situations, friends or even family members choke your vision and dream. Hold on to it and be true to who you are as a person. You are not for everybody and your dream is not for everybody to see, believe or understand. It is your dream.

TOOL 3 - KNOW YOUR GIFTS & USE THEM

What are you afraid of? You were born to contribute something to the planet something that nobody else can. You can do many things. What is the one thing that keeps you awake at night? Why is it that you put more effort into building your boss' vision rather than your own? I'm not suggesting you leave your job, but think about it. If you can stay committed to a forty-hour week and meet targets on a job, you certainly can commit to focusing on your gifts and talents. If you can bake, then I say bake. If you can sing, then I say sing. If you can write, then I say write. Nothing was created by God without a purpose, without a gift, without a talent to do something. Do what is yours to do.

TOOL 4 - FIGHT FEAR

Replace fear with faith. Work your faith muscle and it will work for you. Your faith root must be deep. As you look to your purpose and as you look to your life's work, it becomes necessary to identify fear quickly and replace it. Don't be so quick to quit during adversity. Every time you go through a process, know the purpose of it. The process prepares you with the power to push into divine destiny. It is essential to master the breaking point. After the breaking comes the breaking. In the parable of the 5 loaves and two fish, the loaf multiplied after God broke it. Every single time you face fear, remember that God worked it out the last time. Use your faith as fuel to move forward.

TOOL 5 - CIRCLE UP WITH THE RIGHT PEOPLE

Before God started His three year ministry, one of the first things He did was recruit his team members, His inner circle, and His disciples. I know you might be thinking, but Judas betrayed Him. Guess what? He had to because that was his purpose.

Have the right people in your circle. There are countless studies that have shown that over 80% of successful people were successful because of the team they had. Who is on your team? Do they grow you or stunt you? Are they cynical and negative or do they offer a positive outlook? Be clear about your team.

Bad team members will have you losing every match you enter. Michael Jordan is a great basketball player but he would not be the greatest of all time, had it not been for a strong team. Team up with the right people and get rid of the wrong ones.

As far as negative people go, my advice is love them, pray for them and help them once the opportunity presents itself. Not because you want to but because it's what God requires of you. But for the sake of your purpose and for the sake of your life's work get them off your team and out of your immediate circle.

The minute you recognize a team member is staunchly against the vision or out of alignment, learn the lesson and move on. Circle UP!! And when you find the right team, understand that you are no better than your team. Choose your team based on your task. Choose your team carefully. You are a result of the people you pick.

TOOL 6 - DEVELOP YOURSELF EVERY SINGLE DAY

I never get comfortable. As a speaker, I am always reading, always studying the art of speaking, always networking, always looking at ways to improve. I understand that the biggest room is the room for improvement. The minute you get complacent, is the minute you lose your edge. Whatever you focus on, whatever your passion is; keep your drive up.

Keep working at improving yourself and stay committed to honing your craft. Network with people who can help you get to next level success. The biography I have on my website now is already old because I am working at transforming myself every single day. Bigger and better every day. My roots are anchored in Christ; that means my fruit is excellence, because He is excellent.

Remember the law; from root to fruit. Some ways to develop yourself includes reading books, listening to audios, attending workshops and seminars and networking with successful people.

Never under estimate the power of energy. Low energy people, cynical people, people who lack vision, these are energy drainers. If you want to develop yourself, stay away from them. The draining spirit will drain you too, if you stay around it long enough.

TOOL 7 - WORK SMARTER NEVER HARDER

As you work on your craft, it is important to know who you are. It is equally important to identify a winning strategy. There is no need to reinvent the wheel. Identify one person who is doing exactly what you want to do. Identify a person who is making the level of impact you want to make in the world and understudy them. You don't have to know someone to understudy them. Read their books, listen to their interviews, research their story. Most importantly, study the strategy they utilize to achieve the level of success they have and use it.

TOOL 8 - NEVER DEPEND ON ONE SALARY (MULTIPLE STREAMS OF INCOME)

The vision you have, if it is anything worth doing, I'm assuming it is not small, I am assuming it is not cheap. Everything takes money. God's people are people of excellence and our initiatives should be nothing less than excellent. We are a royal priesthood. Royal dreams and royal visions require royal money. If it is legal and morally correct, use it to create streams of income so that there is money to invest in the vision, in the purpose work and in your life's work.

TOOL 9 - TREAT PEOPLE WELL & SERVE OTHERS

It is important to treat people well and serve others. Who do you serve? If you are only serving yourself, it's going to be hard to get to your destiny. Serve a cause greater than yourself and watch God open the flood gates of heaven for you.

TOOL 10 - TAKE TIME TO APPRECIATE LOVED ONES

Nothing is more important than being present in the moment with loved ones. It is ok to take time away from the vision to enjoy the fruits of your labor. Take time off and take care of you and then take care of them.

TOOL 10 - GRATITUDE JOURNAL

Be thankful for everything. Write seven things down every day that you are grateful for. The soil of gratitude keeps you focused on the vision. Plant yourself in gratitude and remain rooted in it.

TOOL 11 - YOU CAN CHANGE

It's ok to be a different version of yourself than what you and everybody have become accustomed to. You do not have to marry who you know. Commit to transforming something about yourself every day.

TOOL 12 - PRAY AND SPEND TIME WITH GOD

This tool is listed last but it is not least. I wanted to end with it because of how profound this tool is. Your roots need the constant nutrients that come from a deep and personal relationship with God. This is where you get your strength to keep going. Believe it or not, many start the journey, but few make it to the finish line. Life is hard, and it will crush you if you are not rooted in something deeper than your own strength and ability. For me, I am resolute that I must center myself in Him. He keeps me powered, He keeps me planted and He keeps me rooted.

Planted in Purpose Journal Entry
Chapter 6

How do you think each tool can help you on your journey? Write each tool and make it applicable to you. How can you apply it to your daily life?

SALLY ANN GRAY

PLANTED IN PURPOSE

SALLY ANN GRAY

Encouragement from the Author

Have you ever felt lost? Have you ever felt like your life is not where it should be? Do you want to plant yourself in your God given purpose and have a clear direction for your life? When you become planted in your purpose, you are not easily swayed by external circumstances because they are not your source. Your source becomes whatever you are planted in. Ask yourself this, where do my roots get nutrients and water from? That will determine the fruit you see produced in your life. Every plant needs water to live and its big strong roots hold it down in the ground while stretching to the water source, to supply all its needs.

As we know, every plant cannot survive a hurricane. The fact is, not every tree has strong roots. Some trees break when a strong wind passes through. Others are unmovable because their roots go deep in the earth. Similarly, we should want to be so planted in our purpose that nothing and no one can distract us. I developed an acronym for **PLANTED** to keep you encouraged as you work on your purpose.

P- stands for Peace, Be at peace in your purpose and be at home in it. Be patient in the season you are in, be persistent and persevere. Do not judge your purpose based on the season your tree is in right now. For if you can't praise through your winter, you certainly will not make it to your spring. If you make it through the difficult times of your purpose work, better times are sure to come. Go through the process so you can advance to another season of your purpose.

L- stands for Love. Love your purpose. Do not pray for or wish for someone else's purpose. Learn to love what God has given you to do. You cannot succeed at being somebody else and you cannot execute someone else's purpose. Do what is yours to do.

A- stands for All. Give it your All. Be active and do something every day to see God's purpose for your life actualized. If you are truly planted in your purpose, you give it ALL you have. 1st Corinthians 15:58 tells us, *Therefore, my beloved brethren, be ye steadfast, unmovable, **always** abounding in the work of the Lord, forasmuch as ye know that your labor is not in vain in the Lord.* So that tells us, if it is in something else, it will be in vain. Go above and beyond for God.

N- Stands for No. No to ungodly counsel. People who are planted in divine purpose operate in Godly wisdom. Therefore, they are not seeking advice from the world. Say NO to false doctrine. Any advice that is contrary to God's word is a no no.

T- Stands for True. Stay true to your purpose. Stay true to what God has given you. Stay true to the vision. Do not do anything outside of what God has placed in your heart.

E- Stands for Eager. Be eager to do God's will. Always seeking His will for your life and not your own.

D- Stands for delight. Delight yourself in God's plan for your life. Every now and again, your flesh will determine its agenda but when you are planted in purpose, fleshly desire must be rejected. If you are firmly planted, purpose drives you and not your feelings.

To be planted in your purpose means you are unmovable, especially in a storm. Anyone can stand firm when things are going well, and the purpose is unfolding smoothly. Not everyone can stand firm when everything is working against them. To be planted, means that you do not allow the situations on the outside, such as wind, rain or snow, which stands for varying forms of opposition, to blow you off course. External circumstances should not distract you from your purpose.

Another dimension of being planted is staying rooted during life seasons. When God plants you in your purpose, whatever it is, you cannot just move because you feel like. The process is what gives you power. My generation - millennials - as we are called, are very gifted and talented. I am finding that many of us want praise without process. I know it's true, because I was once there, and I have observed it with others in my age group. But what God revealed to me is we must work on the purpose, even without accolades from men. We must be planted and rooted in the things that God gives us to do, even if it's not where we want to be. It is essential to praise through our lows, so we can appreciate our highs. The process is what builds character for the higher season of our purpose.

Be planted in every season, be it good or bad and appreciate it all. Do not judge your life or anyone else's based on the season you see now. Plant yourself in God, plant yourself in His word, and plant yourself in His divine purpose for your life.

Do not judge the outcome of your purpose based on how your tree looks today, for each season serves its due purpose. Understand that your purpose will not bloom during the winter, but you must work during the winter to see flowers in the spring. The real prize is not the flowers that bloom in the spring, the prize is who you become during the winter when there are no flowers visible on the outside. That is when God is working on your roots. I encourage you to push through the difficult times because a better season will come if you stay faithful, if you stay rooted and if you stay planted.

PLANTED IN PURPOSE

Contributors Section

I asked the following women to share their perspective on what it means to truly be planted and rooted in their God-given purpose. I pray that what they share will be a blessing to you.

Kedesha Dallas Goode BA.,MBA., Dip. ED

Author :: Creative :: Educator :: Speaker

What does it mean to be planted in purpose?

At this point in my life when I hear the word 'purpose', I think about our existence here on earth, by extension I view purpose as the gifts and talents that God has blessed each of us with. These unique gifts and talents should consistently and practically illuminate from our life to effect positive change in people's lives, situations and struggles.

Discovery to purpose is not a 'one size fits all' phenomenon; instead it is a gradual learning curve that fits, looks and feels differently for everyone. As your efforts unfold into pockets of breakthrough moments that reflect fulfillment, you will begin to realize what satisfies, empowers and energizes you to persevere towards solidifying your mission related to your purpose. When you recognize what you are built for, you will automatically activate your true purpose. That activation will create a ripple effect of effort, determination, discipline and voila! This combination will slowly but surely plant you into the purpose that God has placed in your being.

When I was exposed to Spanish as a young child, I quickly caught on to the language because my teacher was encouraging and my knack towards the language propelled my efforts to hone my skill thus allowing me to improve at every level. When I decided to do a degree in Spanish, my father wasn't sold on the idea because it didn't conform to the orthodox professions of medicine, law or architecture. I didn't know it was one of my calling or should I say God's purpose for my life, but I pressed forward because I truly love it. Although I recognized my love for the language I never imagined that it would evolve into a full-blown career with so many branches of success, exposure and opportunities. My drive to excel and broaden my horizons has given me the opportunity to study in Spain, Puerto Rico, and France. I am a Foreign Language Educator & Entrepreneur teaching both Spanish and French at all levels and for all qualifications. I didn't know my purpose, but as I held on to my interest and skill I became more vulnerable to my purpose. From then, I became planted into that purpose with determination, consistency, discipline and most importantly prayer. Now that I am emotionally competent and in tune to my God given purposes I have to purposefully mind my mental health so that my roots are being nourished and fed with positive and Christ filled affirmations so that negativity will not take residence and dictate my actions. My advice to you, when you recognize your aptitude towards something, seek God's direction to position your path to seize opportunities that will eventually maximize your talent into soaring success.

Thanks to be to God, I am purposefully made and planted in His promises.

A huge thank you to my friend and sister in Christ, Sally Ann for giving me the opportunity to contribute to this body of work. I know this book will awaken people's interest to discover their purpose(s) and subsequently plant themselves in God's will so that their purpose(s) will materialize to maximize their growth.

Madlyn L. Griffin (Deaconess)

Educational Technician at Joint Base Charleston, SC

Owner/Director of Little Angels Childcare

I would like to say it is an honor and a pleasure to have been asked to complete this task by my sister SallyAnn Gray. First, I prayed and asked God to give me what I need to share about your second book entitled, "Planted In Purpose." I always knew the Lord had a purpose for me. As a believer in Christ, it is God's will for me to do the work He has already shown for me to do. There is a scripture that comes to mind about doing the work, which is, **James 2:17 which states, "In the same way, faith by itself, If it is not accompanied by action, it is dead."** I remember having a conversation with "Sal" about purpose and she said, *"You have to renew your mind, so you will be able to live a purpose filled life, and fulfillment comes from within."* That conversation has been a part of my mind and for sure it was time for me to walk in my "God Given Purpose." Those words have stuck with me until now. Before this conversation, I was nervous and unsure about walking in my purpose. Also, I remember a message my Pastor, John T. Miller preached, which was titled, *"If you have a pulse, you* *have purpose."* With God, Faith and His Spirit guiding me, I'm able to live life with purpose.

Planted in Purpose is knowing your self-worth and allowing God to order your footsteps, so that you will be blessed. I know I'm planted in Purpose because God gave me a vision and He speaks to me on a regular basis about my vision. I find myself hearing things about His vision and without a doubt, I know it is "Him," speaking and dealing with me. He places people and the smallest things in my path, to let me know He's there to help me fulfill the purpose and vision He has for me. I find that He is an on time God. Rather it's at Church, in my home, on the job, driving on the highway, or in the shower, that's where the seeds are being planted in me for me by God. However, He continues to tell me, "Trust the Process." With all that has come to pass and how the Lord has been dealing with me and His vision, I truly believe that it is "The Lord" who is "Feeding My Roots." Scripture tells me in **Psalms 1:3, *That we are like a tree planted by streams of water, which yields its fruit in season and whose leaf does not wither whatever they do prospers.*"** I want to be that tree planted by that stream. So, I encourage you all to build an intimate relationship with our Lord and Savior Jesus Christ and your roots will be fed. God Bless and I pray this testimony blesses whoever reads it!

Wanda Miller

First Lady Emanuel Baptist Church

Psalms 1:3
She is like a tree planted beside the streams
of water that bears its fruit in season
and whose leaves do not wither.
Whatever she does prospers.

My name is Wanda Miller and I am the First Lady, the wife of John T. Miller, Pastor of Emanuel Baptist Church in Summerville, SC, a mother of 5, grandmother of 2, and the Deputy Fire Marshal for a local 200+ Fire Department.

"Planted in Purpose" to me means being rooted and grounded in a specific position in order to fulfill the call that GOD has placed on my life. My purpose is to bring Glory to GOD and GOD alone. It is the true meaning of "Living your Best Now".

Most people know what their purpose in life is. We know that our purpose was given by GOD to glorify GOD, but more times than not, we fail to be "Planted in Purpose" which makes it impossible to fully live out our GOD given purpose and live out our best GOD given lives. We fail to give GOD the time or space to work through us and cultivate that purpose thus making us ineffective for the kingdom of GOD. We become so overwhelmed with things, especially "Church Work" (i.e. being on the choir(s), the praise team, the dance team, this ministry, or that ministry) that we fail to spend the much needed time to receive all that we need from the LORD to ensure our effectiveness for the Kingdom. We are so busy working in the building that we neglect the building, **"You"** cultivating a true relationship with GOD.

We have all be given the great commission of Matt 28:19 to go and make disciples but we cannot do that if we (1) don't have enough WORD in us and the Spirit of GOD leading, guiding, directing and bringing to remembrance that WORD and we (2) cannot climb a flight of stairs to minister that WORD.

My GOD-given purpose is to help Women, young or old, married or single develop and lead lives that make us both, first Spiritually and then Physically, 'Fit to Be Used by GOD". I encourage ladies to seek first the kingdom of GOD believing that everything else will be added. Not looking at tradition or religion that creates barriers, boundaries and limitations but rather seeking and cultivating a relationship with our FATHER and CREATOR, the lover of our souls which comes with limitless possibilities for an abundant and fulfilling life. I care about how you view yourself and I especially care about your relationship with GOD because I wholeheartedly believe that how you view yourself is deeply dependent on your relationship with GOD. The only way a person, no matter what their stature, can see themselves the way GOD sees them is having a relationship with GOD. By helping then build the most important and most beneficial relationship they could ever have will help them discover, cultivate, better equip them to walk in their GOD-given purpose.

I believe that while GOD wants a Spiritually trained willing vessel (2 Timothy 2:21 If a man therefore purge himself from these, he shall be a vessel unto honor, sanctified, and meet for the master's use, [and] prepared unto every good work.) HE also needs an Physically able vessel (1 Corinthians 6:19-20 Or do you not know that your body is a temple of the Holy Spirit within you, whom you have from God? You are not your own, for you were bought with a price. So glorify God in your body.) Keeping in mind that our goal for exercise should never be to improve the quality of our bodies so that other people will notice and admire us. Rather, the goal of exercising should be to improve our physical health so we will possess more physical energy and the physical ability to carry out Spiritual calls and duties.

Alderene Young

Educator

I was seeking God in prayer concerning an unrelated issue to what I am about to discuss and the Holy Spirit said "Write now," and immediately I heard focus on the "willow tree". Not knowing anything about this plant I decided embark on a research. This tree loves water and spreads its roots in an effort to locate any water source or grows in the direction of the existing water in the soil. Amazingly these roots will travel as far as 40 feet to reach a water source or water rich soils. The willow's roots are a distinct example of how we are expected to operate in our Christian walk. The willow's ultimate goal is to seek only one source and that is water. The where, the when and the how are not questions of necessity because it's a "Must have"; notwithstanding any consequences, repercussions or concerns about what may act as hindrances in its path. This water has to be reached by any means necessary. It is advised that when planting a willow tree it has to be ensured that utility poles as well as other grounded object are not located in that environment. The expectation of the people of God is to stay connected to the Holy Spirit and seek the source of our life, our living water Jesus at all times. Psalm 34: 1 says that

"I will praise the Lord at all times, his praise shall continually be in my mouth." This is a clear indication that like the willow we should be seeking our source continuously which is Jesus. The devil devises a new plan daily to destroy God's people and we cannot win these spiritual battles if we are not walking in the spirit. John 4:24 (KJV) outlines clearly that

"God is a Spirit: and they that worship him must worship him in spirit and in truth". 2 Corinthians 10:3-5 King (KJV) substantiates this by telling us that "though we walk in the flesh, we do not war after the flesh:(For the weapons of our warfare are not carnal, but mighty through God to the pulling down of strong holds;) Casting down imaginations, and every high thing that exalted itself against the knowledge of God, and bringing into captivity every thought to the obedience of Christ". These scriptures clarifies the need for God as our source, hence the need to stay connected to him like the Willow is connected to its own water source. They also emphasize the need to acknowledge that our Christian walk is spiritual and so if we say we are rooted, we have to be walking a spiritual walk and talking a spiritual talk. The directives of how we are expected to do this is indicated in Galatians 5:16-26 (KJV) "This I say then, Walk in the Spirit, and ye shall not fulfil the lust of the flesh. For the flesh lusted against the Spirit, and the Spirit against the flesh: and these are contrary the one to the other: so that ye cannot do the things that ye would. But if ye be led of the Spirit, ye are not under the law. Now the works of the flesh are manifest, which are these; Adultery, fornication, uncleanness, lasciviousness, Idolatry, witchcraft, hatred, variance, emulations, wrath, strife, seditions, heresies, Envying, murders, drunkenness, reveling, and such like: of which I tell you before, as I have also told you in time past, that they which do such things shall not inherit the kingdom of God. But the fruit of the Spirit is love, joy, peace, longsuffering, gentleness, goodness, faith, Meekness, temperance: against such there is no law. And they that are Christ's have crucified the flesh with the affections and lusts. If we live in the Spirit, let us also walk in the Spirit. Let us not be desirous of vain glory, provoking one another, envying one another"

Verses 16 and 17 highlights that there is continued conflict between the flesh and the spirit and clarifies that when you are rooted in the spirit you cannot do the things that your flesh desires. Verses 18 through to 26 gives a distinct separation of the lusts of the flesh as well as the fruits of the spirit. Just like the willow tree with its roots exposed at its trunk the world is looking at us as children of God. Matthew 17: 15 – 20 says that by their fruits you shall know them. Hence as children of God our roots should always be connected to our source so that we do not exhibit the lusts of the flesh but at all times everything about us should be a reflection of the fruits of the spirit. Keep your roots reaching for and connected to the source which is Christ Jesus.

Genee Kinsey

Singer / Songwriter / Worship Leader

To be planted in purpose means to be rooted and grounded in God's perfect plan for Genee's life. I know that, if I seek the Kingdom of God first, and His righteousness, then everything else that I need will be provided. I choose to trust God in ALL things concerning me and it has not failed me yet. He is my source, strength and my very foundation; and it is in HIM that I live, move and have my being.

Therefore, I am confident through Christ. When I am faced with the issues of life, trials and tribulations, I have to remind myself of my foundation, my roots, where I came from, who my Father is and what He can do; who He told me that I was and all that I have inherited as His child. I understand that He created me for HIS purpose and, as long as I allow God to order my steps, stay focused on Him and do what He instructs me to do, then I will remain planted in His Purpose.

Crystal Daye

Award-Winning Author/ Inspirational Speaker/ International Christian Coach and Dynamic Entrepreneur

"There must be more to life than work, pay bills and die" – I found myself thinking about this for months. I had acquired all the things I was told I needed to accomplish to live a happy life. I had the house, the car, the child, engaged to get married, good job, education… I felt it was selfish to even want more. But, for some reason I kept hearing "you are made for more Crystal". There was a deeper longing for more; not more things or not to do more, but to be more. As this desire deepen, I knew the more I was searching for, could not be filled by me or by acquiring more "things"; I knew only the true and living God, Creator of the universe could fulfill this longing.

Sitting at a new years eve party, in my heart I cried out to God and said I surrender. This surrender didn't start there and certainly didn't end there, but I believe the mind shift happened that night because all the things I thought was fun no longer appealed to me. My pursuit of purpose began. I sought a relationship with God intentionally and I gave myself to Him, He revealed more and more the purpose He placed me on this earth for.

Purpose comes from pain. Purpose comes from passion. Purpose comes through perseverance. God used my messes, my tests, my desires and my gifts to plant me in His purpose and influence many lives. Today, I speak boldly, I write confidently, I coach passionately, I teach authentically and I serve faithfully. I've watched God truly using my gifts to make room for me and impact many lives all over the world. Now, I help others share their message by writing books and becoming speakers, building their income through coaching and launching businesses and most importantly walking courageously in their calling to also impact the kingdom of God.

Being planted in purpose has brought true joy, peace, fulfillment and happiness to my life but also to the lives of anyone who comes in contact with me.

Crystal Daye, Award-Winning Author, Inspirational Speaker, International Christian Coach and Dynamic Entrepreneur and mother of Christelle. As the COO of DayeLight Publishers and Christian Coaches Alliance, she is passionate about helping Christ-centered individuals to clarity their message, birth their books and build profitable brands and businesses. Find out more at www.crystaldaye.com or email info@crystaldaye.com

Shakobie Butler

Special Educator

Speaker

What does it mean to you to be planted in purpose in Christ?

When I think of the person who is "Planted in Purpose", I am reminded of Psalm 1:3 which says, "And he shall be like a tree planted by the rivers of water, that bringeth forth his fruit in his season; his leaf also shall not wither; and whatsoever he doeth shall prosper". To be planted is to be grounded and immovable from your relationship with the Father, Son and Holy Spirit. Things good or bad cannot sway you from their presence, but they push you deeper into their presence because of their tremendous goodness!

For me, being planted in purpose is moving forward when what I see does not line up with what I know God has spoken. God spoke and created the very earth on which I live, so I am confident that even when I don't see the fullness of His promise, it is already done just because He spoke it! Just like the tree, as I continue to allow my roots to go deeper and draw from the rivers of Living Water, I can be assured that in season I will continue to bear much fruit and prosper in all that I have been called to do!

Sherie Nelson-Allen

Educator, Life Coach in Training

Planted in Purpose

To be planted in purpose is to experience lack of dissonance, to be grounded in harmony with your values, to find peace and contentment with your who, what, where and how.

Planted in purpose means you are connected to who you are, your life and journey, and using it to bless others. It also focuses on where you are in life, it is a journey of understanding where you have been, where you are now and how you will continuously strive to improve yourself as well as those around you. In finding your what (what do you want out of your journey) it helps you to know who you are.

I believe my primary purpose is to help others in life to experience harmony in their lives, and to help them find purpose as we are all on this journey together.

When you are planted in purpose, everything becomes aligned and you experience total clarity on your life journey.

Final Message from the Author

Thank you for taking the time to read this book. I pray it has blessed you. I pray that you have experienced a shift. I pray that you will come into direct alignment with God's perfect will for your life. I pray that you will apply every nugget, every pocket of wisdom, every strategy, every law and every principle to achieving your goals. I pray that you use the tools I have shared to become planted and remain rooted in your God-given purpose. I am using them right alongside you to remain rooted in mine. In the journal pages that follow, I ask that you document how you have planted yourself in your purpose. If this book has helped you to become planted and rooted in purpose, I would love to hear from you. Please send an email to sallyanngrayspeaks@outlook.com or visit my website at www.sallyanngrayspeaks.com to leave a testimonial.

SallyAnn Gray

God Bless

As you prepare to document your journey of walking in purpose, I ask that you declare these BOLD declarations over your life. I ask that you journal your thoughts, goals, commitments and action steps for the next twenty-one days.

- I AM PLANTED IN PURPOSE
- I AM ROOTED IN CHRIST
- I HAVE VALUE
- I AM FEARFULLY AND WONDERFULLY MADE
- I CAN DO ALL THINGS THROUGH CHRIST WHO GIVES ME STRENGTH

SALLY ANN GRAY

TWENTY-ONE DAY JOURNAL ENTRY CHALLENGE

DAY 1

DAY 2

DAY 3

DAY 4

DAY 5

DAY 6

DAY 7

DAY 8

DAY 9

DAY 10

DAY 11

DAY 12

DAY 13

DAY 14

DAY 15

DAY 16

DAY 17

DAY 18

DAY 19

DAY 20

DAY 21

www.ingramcontent.com/pod-product-compliance
Lightning Source LLC
Chambersburg PA
CBHW052149110526
44591CB00012B/1909